What If Tomorrow Never Comes?

If tomorrow is the question, Let this be the answer

Ryna Raheja

BookLeaf
Publishing

India | USA | UK

Made with ❤ on the BookLeaf Publishing Platform
www.bookleafpub.in
www.bookleafpub.com

Dedication

To Neeha ma'am,

*You always urged us to read, to lose ourselves in words
and find meaning
between the lines.*

*Perhaps I turned the pages too late, but some lessons
never fade.*

So let this be the credit long overdue;

*To the one who didn't just teach words, but gave them
meaning.*

Preface

Some moments slip through the cracks, gone before they can be held. Others leave their fingerprints on time, refusing to fade. This book is a collection of the softness of beginnings, the sting of change, the hands that shaped us, the love that burned and healed, and the goodbyes that never really meant *gone*.

Each page carries echoes of growth, loss, nostalgia, and quiet gratitude.

Maybe, just maybe, you'll find pieces of yourself here too, hidden between the lines, waiting to be felt…

Acknowledgements

Acknowledged are none, yet the whispers of everything and everyone around me echo through these pages...

Chapter 1: Love Was a Language We Didn't Have to Learn

Before we knew what love meant, we already felt it. It wasn't in grand gestures or carefully chosen words—it was in the way someone tucked a blanket around us when we fell asleep, the warmth of a familiar voice calling our name, the unspoken understanding in a shared glance. This chapter isn't about the kind of love that needed definitions. It's about the kind that simply existed;effortless, unshaken, and unquestioned.

1. The Arms That Felt Like Home

They never asked for thank-yous,
never needed promises in return.
Love was laced into late-night lullabies,
woven into hands that caught every fall.

Laughter spilled onto tiled floors,
echoing through the years untouched.
Safety wasn't a place back then,
it was a heartbeat close enough to hear.

We didn't question it, never thought to.
The world felt big, but not too big,
because someone was always there;
steady, certain, waiting.

2. The Universe Outside the Door

The door stood open, silent and wide,
a world beyond, too vast to hide.
Fingers curled against the frame,
feet unmoving, stuck the same.

The voices called, soft yet strong,
the road ahead was far and long.
The sky stretched high, the air ran free,
yet something whispered, stay with me.

The door remained, it never closed,
its warmth still wrapped in golden glow.
Not left behind, not lost for good,
just waiting there, as home should.

3. The Sky Was Never the Limit

Feet on the ground, eyes on the sky,
chasing the clouds as they drifted by.
Dreams flew past through the restless trees,
carried away by a wandering breeze.

They murmured, *"Go slow, stay in line,"*
but the stars sang, *"You were born to shine."*

The road stretched far, the path unknown,
some journeys are best when walked alone.

Step by step, the world grew small,
but the sky was never a limit at all.
Feet kept moving, fears turned light,
even the dark could not steal the flight.

4. The Unwritten Pages

A book lay open, waiting still,
craving the ink, the poet's will.
Fingers hovered, a quiet doubt,
"What if the words don't quite spill out?"

The page just stared, blank and wide,
a restless ocean, a silent tide.
"What if the story strays too far?"
"What if the ink forgets its spark?"

But pages are not meant to stay pristine,
they long for chaos, for in-between.
So the ink ran wild, the hands let go,
and the unwritten finally flowed.

Chapter 2: The Goodbyes We Didn't Hear Coming

Some goodbyes are loud, wrapped in tears and farewells. But the hardest ones are silent. The friendships, places, and moments we swore would always be there—until one day, they weren't. There was no warning, no dramatic ending. Just a slow fade until we woke up and realized the people who once felt like home had become echoes.

These poems hold the weight of those unnoticed goodbyes—the ones we wish we had seen coming.

5. The Day Before Everything Changed

We didn't know it was our last walk home,
laughing at jokes we'd forget by morning.
Didn't know the way we said " *see you tomorrow* "
was the last time tomorrow would come.

No dramatic ending, no heavy pause,
just a casual wave and a door closing.
No slow-motion goodbye, no final words,
just time pulling us apart like it always does.

We didn't know the world had already shifted,
that we were stepping into the before and after.
That one day, we'd look back and wonder;
how did we not hear the goodbye?

6. Familiar Roads, Unknown Destinations

We walked the same way every day,
past the shop with the broken sign.
The wall we once painted stood tall,
the shortcut we knew felt like ours.

The cracks in the pavement knew us,
the streetlights flickered in greeting.
The trees swayed gently as we passed,
as if they listened to our voices.

It felt like the world stayed the same,
until one day, everything changed.
The shop stood empty in silence,
the wall's colors faded to dust.

Some streets remember our footsteps,
but they don't wait for us to stay.

7. Paper Boats & Unfinished Letters

We folded dreams into paper boats,
and let them drift down rainy streets.
The ink on our palms smudged softly,
as we wrote words we never sent.

"*See you soon,*" but soon never came,
"*Miss you,*" but silence answered back.
The wind carried our unsaid thoughts,
tucking them between falling leaves.

Some letters lay beneath our beds,
their edges curled with quiet time.
Some boats found oceans far away,
but never learned how to return.

We promised the tides would know us,
but even waves forget our names.

8. Unfinished Conversations

"What do you wanna be?" they asked,
between half-eaten lunches and crumpled notes.
"I don't know yet," came the answer,
as if dreams had deadlines to meet.

Names scratched on wooden desks,
forever paired with fading ink.
Some stayed, some disappeared,
like echoes in empty halls.

We spoke of tomorrows like promises,
never thinking they'd slip away.
Now the echoes are all that's left,
words we meant to say.

Chapter 3: Laughter That Still Echoes in Empty Hallways

Some places never forget us. The laughter in classrooms, the scribbled notes, the teachers who believed in us— these moments linger, even when the hallways grow silent. Friendships that felt unbreakable, inside jokes that made no sense outside those walls, and the echoes of a time when the future felt far away. These aren't just memories; they are pieces of us, scattered like chalk dust on an empty blackboard.

9. Traces Of Thoughts

Ink stains linger on empty pages,
side notes whisper what minds won't share.
A half-drawn face, a word underlined,
a thought once clear, now undefined.

Margins filled with questions untold,
letters smudged, their echoes cold.
Did it all matter, or fade in the fray?
Yet the ink remains, refusing to stray.

Scribbled truths, a fleeting mark,
glimpses of souls left in the dark.
Erased by time, but never erased;
every word still holds its place.

10. Chalk Dust & Handprints

White dust lingers on worn-out sleeves,
traces of lessons left behind.
Echoes of voices that shaped the road,
etching belief in doubtful minds.

Red marks on pages, not of shame,
but hands that guided, firm yet kind.
Every scold, a whispered hope,
every push, a place to climb.

The bell rings, the steps move on,
but chalk dust clings like quiet proof—
that someone once believed enough
to leave their mark on you.

11. The Ones Who Knew Before We Did

They saw sparks before they were flames,
mapped out paths we had yet to walk.
In every stumble, they saw a step,
in every doubt, a voice to talk.

Their words were quiet, steady hands,
lifting dreams too shy to rise.
A gentle nudge, a knowing glance,
turning fears to battle cries.

We took our bows, claimed the stage,
forgetting who had set the light.
Yet in the echoes of our names,
their faith still burns, steady and bright.

12. Borrowed & Forgotten

A pencil slipped into open palms,
passed like a quiet promise; never signed,
never sealed, yet understood.

It left no name, no rightful claim,
yet traced letters, solved sums,
sketched dreams on the margins of time.

Some things are lent, never returned,
but maybe that's the point!
to leave a mark, even when gone.

Memories, like graphite, fade too soon,
smudged by time yet never erased.
Somewhere, someone still holds a piece of you,
pressed between pages, waiting to be found.

Chapter 4: When Love Wasn't Forever, But It Was Real

The first heartbreaks—ones that didn't always come from deep affection, but still changed us.

Not all heartbreaks are about love stories. Some come from friendships that slipped through our fingers, dreams that never reached the sky, or moments that felt endless but faded too soon. There were people who felt like home until they didn't, words we never found the courage to say, and places that now feel unfamiliar. Even if they didn't stay, even if they weren't meant to, they were real. And maybe, that's enough.

13. Bridges & Unfinished Letters

We built bridges with whispered promises,
stacked high with laughter and late-night dreams.
Letters half-written, words left unsent,
sealed in envelopes that never found hands.

But bridges burn when hands let go,
and silence turns ink into ghosts.
Somewhere between yesterday and tomorrow,
we lost the tides that once led us home.

Not all endings come with echoes of goodbye,
some just fade like ink on water,
leaving only shadows where we used to stand.

14. The Letters That Never Arrived

A letter to a childhood friend,
sealed with laughter, lost in the wind.
Did they ever wonder too—
where the years disappeared?

A note to a teacher, never sent,
scribbled on a last-page corner.
The "thank you" stayed in ink,
but never in her hands.

A message for the one who left,
typed, deleted, rewritten, erased.
Did they ever check their inbox,
or was it just another ghost?

A postcard for home,
addressed but never mailed.
Sometimes, love feels too big
for an envelope to hold.

15. The Apologies We Gave Without Words

In silence, we shared our deepest regret,
No words spoken, but the message was set.
A glance, a touch, all we needed to say,
Our hearts apologized in the quietest way.

No need for sounds, no grand gestures made,
In the stillness, our remorse softly laid.
Forgiveness found in the silence we keep,
A bond rebuilt, quiet but deep.

In moments unspoken, we found our way,
Apologies linger, where words couldn't stay.

16. The Places We Outgrew Before We Were Ready

We left behind places that held our dreams,
When we weren't ready, or so it seems.
The streets we knew, the corners we loved,
Became too small as we grew above.

The comfort we had, the path we once walked,
Now feels distant, as time has talked.
We left too soon, unsure of the cost,
Of finding ourselves, though something was lost.

Yet in the leaving, we learned to be free,
Embracing the unknown, where we're meant to be.

Chapter 5: Hands That Shaped Us

Some people enter our lives like fleeting shadows, leaving marks we often don't notice at first. These imprints, some light and others heavy, shape the way we grow, think, and feel. It's not always the ones who stayed the longest, but the ones who touched us at the right time. In this chapter, we explore the hands that shaped us; the teachers, the voices, parents, the people who were fleeting chapters in our lives, and the quiet art of leaving without leaving scars. These are the stories of how fingerprints, though invisible, remain etched within us, forever altering the path we walk.

17. The Teachers Who Taught Us More Than Subjects

They didn't just speak with words and sounds,
They opened our minds and broke the bounds.
In their eyes, we saw dreams take flight,
A spark in the dark, a guiding light.

They taught us to question, to look within,
To find strength in failure, to rise again.
Their lessons were woven in moments, not just talk,
In every quiet step, in every long walk.

They gave us the courage to stand, to grow,
To see the world as we've never known.
With hands that shaped us, they left a trace,
A part of them stays, in every space.

18. Ink on Old Notebooks & Voices That Still Echo

Pages worn thin, with thoughts of the past,
In ink, we wrote, hoping they'd last.
The words may fade, but the meaning stays,
Echoing softly through the passing days.

Old notebooks, stained with time's gentle touch,
Hold secrets we learned, the lessons too much.
The voices that spoke, now whispers in air,
Still echo inside, reminding us to care.

They live in the margins, the spaces we left,
In moments imperfect, in feelings unkept.
Though time may erase, and distance may part,
Their ink stays alive, etched deep in the heart.

19. People Who Were Chapters, Not the Whole Book

They came like stories, brief and bright,
A spark in the dark, then out of sight.
Their words were pages, their presence a verse,
A chapter in time, for better or worse.

We lived through their lessons, their smiles, their tears,
But like every story, they disappeared.
Not meant to stay, yet they shaped our way,
Leaving footprints in the dust of yesterday.

They weren't the ending, just part of the plot,
A brief encounter, but never forgot.
For in the chapters they helped us write,
We found our courage, we found our light.

20. The Art of Leaving Without Slamming the Door

They didn't leave with loud goodbyes,
No angry words, no tear-filled eyes.
They left like whispers, soft and kind,
Leaving behind peace of mind.

No slamming doors, no final fight,
Just quiet steps in the fading night.
They knew the art of leaving with grace,
Of knowing when it was time, and the right place.

Their absence wasn't an empty space,
But a quiet shift in life's embrace.
And though they're gone, they left us free,
In the softest way, they let us be.

Chapter 6: The Bonds That Burn & Heal

Love, loss, and the delicate art of healing—this chapter delves into the raw, often painful spaces where our hearts burn, break, and rebuild. In the aftermath of unspoken applause, silent struggles, and fading versions of ourselves, we learn that our worth is not defined by what was lost, but by what remains. Here, we explore the complex dance between fire and healing, the painful yet necessary cycles that shape us. Through the embers of broken bonds, we discover that we are whole, even when things fall apart.

21. The Applause That Never Came

We waited in silence, hearts full of hope,
For applause that never echoed, never spoke.
We gave everything, we gave it all,
Yet the silence grew louder with every fall.

The stage was set, the lights so bright,
But no one saw us in the quiet night.
We reached for recognition, for praise to find,
But the crowd was deaf, the praise left behind.

And yet, in the stillness, we learned to stand,
Not needing applause to understand.
For the worth we sought was never in sound,
But in the strength we built on the ground.

22. Finding Fireflies in the Dark

In the darkest hours, when hope feels thin,
We search for light, for something within.
The world may be silent, the night may fall,
But tiny sparks shine, answering the call.

Like fireflies dancing in the blackest skies,
We find fleeting moments, where the spirit lies.
They flicker softly, they shine so bright,
Guiding us gently through the endless night.

In the stillness of darkness, they teach us to see,
That even in shadows, we can still be free.
For light doesn't always roar, it whispers true,
And fireflies are proof, that light can renew.

23. The Heart That Heals Itself

The heart, a garden bruised by storm,
Seeds of pain take root and form.
Yet in the soil, the rain gives way,
To roots that stretch, and skies that sway.

Wounds like rivers carve the land,
But time, the sun, softens the sand.
The cracks are filled with whispered light,
As shadows fade into the night.

No healer comes with steady hands,
The heart is its own, with hidden plans.
In silence, it grows, as wild winds cease,
For the heart that heals itself finds peace.

24. The Versions of Us That No Longer Exist

We were once stories, painted in gold,
Versions of us, both timid and bold.
We lived in moments, in dreams untold,
But like shifting tides, we couldn't hold.

The faces we wore, the voices we knew,
Are whispers now, lost in the blue.
The hands that once reached, the eyes that once shone,
Are shadows of what we've outgrown.

We shed our skin like old, worn thread,
Leaving behind the parts we once fed.
The versions of us that no longer remain,
Live in memories, both joy and pain.

Chapter 7: The Waves Never Stay, But the Ocean Remembers

Regret lingers like the ebb and flow of the tide, soft yet persistent. Nostalgia wraps us in its arms, pulling us back to moments that feel distant yet strangely close. In this chapter, we explore the gentle reminders that though the waves may crash and retreat, the ocean carries every trace. The things we think we've lost, the words unsaid, and the chapters unfinished—they are never truly gone. They remain within us, echoes carried by the current.

25. The Tides Took Us, But Left Our Names Behind

The tide pulls back, the footprints fade,
The shore we stood on, now far away.
We walked with certainty, hearts unshaken,
Not knowing which moments would be forsaken.

The ocean whispers in restless waves,
Carrying echoes of things we gave.
It holds the laughter, the salt of tears,
The weight of our stories across the years.

But we, the wanderers, drift too fast,
Forgetting the shores we thought would last.
Only when silence meets the sea,
Do we wonder; was it us, or them, who left first?

26. The Silence After the Last Bell

The last bell rang, but we didn't hear,
Lost in the hum of one more year.
We packed our bags, we walked away,
Not knowing we'd never return the same way.

Laughter still lingers in hollowed halls,
Scattered like echoes against the walls.
Not all goodbyes are spoken loud—
Some slip away beneath the crowd.

By the time we turned to look behind,
The world had shifted, rewrote the lines.
We thought we had time, we thought we would stay,
But some last times never feel that way.

27. Pages We Didn't Get to Write

Some stories ended before they began,
left unfinished by time's quiet hand.
Words hung in the air, half-formed,
sentences waiting to be born.

A book left open, spine unbent,
chapters we dreamed but never spent.
Ink that dried before it could flow,
letters unspoken, lost in the glow.

Not every story finds its end,
some just linger, some pretend.
But even in silence, they still exist,
pressed between pages we'll always miss.

28. The Echo of Names We No Longer Say

Some names rest on the tip of the tongue,
soft as whispers, heavy as stone.
Once spoken like second nature,
now left untouched, unknown.

They linger in the spaces between,
woven into songs we no longer sing.
A syllable almost spoken,
a ghost in the air, fleeting, broken.

Not forgotten, not erased,
just waiting in the quiet place
where echoes live and letters fade,
and names still call, though none remain.

Chapter 8: The Weight of What Stays

Letting go does not mean losing. Some things remain— woven into us like old songs, carried in the quiet corners of memory. We move forward, yet some places, some lessons, some people stay with us, no matter how far we go.

Not everything fades with time. Some moments settle in our bones, whispering their presence long after we have left them behind.

29. Ghosts of Places We Called Home

Some places stay beneath our skin,
no matter how far we have gone.
Their walls still hum with voices lost,
their echoes never fully gone.

The air still holds the weight of us,
as if we never walked away.
Not every ghost is meant to haunt,
some simply ask us not to stray.

They live in songs we used to love,
in scents that take us back in time.
A doorway passed a thousand times,
yet still, it feels like crossing lines.

30. Lessons That Didn't Come Easy

Some truths arrived with quiet steps,
while others knocked down every door.
We learned that silence speaks the loudest,
and some goodbyes aren't meant for war.

We held on tight to hands that shook,
mistook the cracks for something whole.
Not every lesson came so gently,
some carved their mark into our soul.

But even wounds can turn to wisdom,
even losses light the way.
What broke us once now stands beside us,
a lesson learned, but not erased.

31. What We Keep in the Spaces They Leave

They leave, but never empty-handed,
something of them always stays.
A laugh tucked into old voicemails,
a name we flinch at when it's played.

A seat still pulled out at the table,
a habit we don't break in time.
Their favorite song still hums within us,
like second nature, like a sign.

We fill the gaps with quiet echoes,
with what was said, with what was not.
Some spaces stay, not as absence,
but as proof of what we've lost.

32. The Things That Stayed Anyway

They left, but their stories didn't.
Their words still knock at the door.
We don't call their names out loud,
but they linger in the air we ignore.

Their jokes still slip into laughter,
their footsteps still creak in the floor.
We stopped waiting for them to return,
but never asked them to leave for sure.

Not everything leaves when it should.
Not every goodbye is complete.
Some people fade from our lives,
but never quite from our reach.

Chapter 9: We Became Stories & That Was Enough

The acceptance that nothing truly disappears—some things just become stories instead. The people who shaped us, the moments that changed us, the love that didn't last but still meant something.

We carry them, not in our hands, but in the way we remember, the way we speak, the way we keep them alive in stories.

33. The Way We Live On in the Minds of Others

We are more than echoes that fade with the wind,
more than footsteps erased by the turning tide.
We stay in the songs that once made us dance,
in words we once spoke that now feel like theirs.

We stay in the habits they never unlearned,
in laughter that sounds like we are still near.
We stay in the silence before saying our name,
in memories carried through all of the years.

Time may reshape how our presence remains,
but we are still here in the lives that we touched.

34. Memories Are Just Time Travel in Disguise

A polaroid fades, but never truly disappears,
holding smiles frozen in soft, hazy light.
Videos play like echoes of yesterday,
voices reaching across the years.

Old messages wait in quiet corners,
words untouched, but never unread.
Photographs whisper stories to the silence,
turning moments into something endless.

Time moves forward, but memories resist,
rewinding, replaying—bringing you back.

35. We Were Here, and That's Enough

Not every story is carved in stone,
some live in the spaces between whispers.
Not every name is etched in history,
some are simply spoken with love.

Footprints fade, but the steps we took remain,
leading forward, shaping the path.
Even if time forgets the details,
the feeling of us lingers in the air.

We were here, even if the world moves on,
and maybe that's enough;
to have existed, to have mattered,
to have been a part of something worth remembering.

36. Some Things End, But We Carry Them Still

A key with no lock, a number never dialled,
a song we skip but never delete.
Some endings don't ask for permission,
they just slip between the cracks of yesterday.

But even when places forget our footsteps,
we still carry the weight of being there.
Not in the way we once did,
but in the way a scent brings back a season,
or how a familiar street still knows our name.

Some things end, but they don't vanish;
they just learn to exist without being seen.

Chapter 10: The Sky Still Holds All Our Tomorrows

Hope is not just the flicker of light at the end of a tunnel; it is the quiet certainty that the sun will rise, even after the longest night. Some stories may end, but life keeps turning its pages, carrying us forward, whether we are ready or not. In the echoes of what once was, we find strength; in the unknown of tomorrow, we find possibility. This chapter is a reminder that even when we can't see the way ahead, the sky still holds all our tomorrows, waiting for us to step into them.

37. The Sun Rises Even After the Darkest Nights

The night stretches long, its silence heavy,
Stars flicker like whispers too tired to stay.
But even when shadows linger the longest,
The sun still finds its way back to the day.

Storms may shatter what once felt certain,
Winds may carry pieces we cannot chase.
Yet morning comes with golden defiance,
Painting the sky in light's warm embrace.

Not every loss is the end of the story,
Not every sorrow is meant to last.
The sun rises, as it always has,
Turning yesterday into the past.

38. Wounds Turn Into Stories, Stories Turn Into Strength

The door stood open, silent and wide,
a world beyond, too vast to hide.
Fingers curled against the frame,
feet unmoving, stuck the same.

The voices called, soft yet strong,
the road ahead was far and long.
The sky stretched high, the air ran free,
yet something whispered, stay with me.

The door remained, it never closed,
its warmth still wrapped in golden glow.
Not left behind, not lost for good,
just waiting there, as home should.

39. One Day, We'll Look Back & Smile

The nights that felt too heavy to carry,
The days that blurred in shades of gray,
Will one day rest as quiet echoes,
Softly calling from far away.

The storms we feared would never leave,
Will turn to mist in morning light.
What seemed too vast to ever conquer,
Will shrink in distance, lost from sight.

And when we stand where time has led us,
With gentler hearts and lighter hands,
We'll see those days not as our breaking,
But as the steps that let us stand.

40. The Sky Remembers

The road ahead is laced with questions,
But the sky still holds the sun's return.
The past may whisper, soft and aching,
Yet new horizons call and burn.

The stars we lost still shine above us,
Though distant now, they light the way.
The winds may shift, the seasons falter,
But dawn still comes: come what may.

So even when the night feels endless,
And every step is laced with sorrow,
Look up—the sky still stands unbroken,
Still holding all our bright tomorrows.

A Chapter That Isn't Numbered

Phew! This book took *forever* to come together. Not because I didn't want to write it, but because I'm a *hop-here-hop-there* kind of person. My brain is always five steps ahead, my heart is still lingering in yesterday, and somehow, my hands managed to put it all into words.

I'm an AS-level student, which means I exist in that weird space where people call me mature for my age, but I still feel like I'm just figuring things out. I don't think I know everything—I just see life from too many angles at once. Maybe I don't always show it, but I do.

This book? It's full of goodbyes, nostalgia, and memories —the things we all try to avoid thinking about until we have no choice. But I believe they deserve the same weight as our happiest moments. Maybe even more. Because happiness is easy to carry, but nostalgia? That's the one we tuck away in the quiet corners of our hearts.

I get attached too easily; to friends, to family, to teachers. Surprisingly, I talk to my teachers more than I talk to my friends. I go to school, not just for academics, but for the feeling of home it gives me. Attachments are beautiful, but they come with a cost. The deeper you hold on, the harder it is to let go.

I pray when I see angel numbers. I close my eyes at 11:11 and make wishes I never say out loud.
I used to believe that *God is one*, but now I believe *God is the one.* The one I turn to when I'm lost. The one I go to when I don't know where else to go.

I keep Polaroids like proof that time once stood still for me. I write long messages and letters to the people I love. (*If you've ever received one, just know, I meant every word.*)

And in the days I've been writing this book, I've learned something that no one really talks about...
We don't value people enough while they're still here.
We assume we'll have more time.
But time doesn't give warnings. It just moves forward, with or without us.

That's probably why I love photography and videography so much. They let me hold on to the things that time tries to erase. I want to capture moments before they slip through my fingers. To frame the laughter, the quiet glances, the way the sunlight hits someone's face at just the right angle. Maybe that's my way of fighting against the inevitable; by making sure that even if moments fade, they're never truly gone.

To My Family...

My parents—there will never be enough words to capture what you mean to me. You have been my strongest supporters, my safe place. Everything I am today is because of the love, the lessons, and the unwavering belief you've had in me. You've given me the freedom to dream, to explore, to make mistakes, and to find my way back home. I hope, one day, I can be even half the person you have been to me.

My sisters & my brothers—you are my built-in best friends, my lifelong partners in crime. We fight, we tease, we annoy each other endlessly, but at the end of the day, I wouldn't trade you for the world. No matter where life takes us, I know we'll always have each other.

More of my family—you are the ones who fill my life with stories and laughter. You are my roots, my connection to something bigger than myself. Your presence in my life is a reminder that family isn't just about the people we are born to, but about those who stand by us through it all.

To My Teachers...

You all have given me more than just lessons inside a classroom. You have shaped the way I think, the way I see the world, and most importantly, the way I see myself. You have taught me that learning isn't just about textbooks and exams; it's about curiosity, about questioning, about never settling for less than my full potential.

And to my English teacher,

There was a time I didn't truly value what it meant to be taught by you. When you stood at the front of the classroom, when your words filled the air, I didn't fully grasp what it was—the feeling of being taught *by you*. But now, I know. Now, I understand what I had, and what it means to have had a teacher like you.

Since I've started expressing myself more, you have listened to me in ways that I never expected, and for that, I am truly grateful. You have been more than just an educator; you have been a guiding light, a source of warmth, a reminder that kindness and wisdom can change lives.

And to my other teachers, I wish I could name each of you and thank you personally, but if I did, it would be quite a challenge... however, thank you for being the kind of mentors who make learning more than just a subject. You've challenged me, encouraged me, and made me believe in my own abilities. You've left a lasting impact on my journey, and I will always be grateful.

To My Friends...

To the ones who have laughed with me, cried with me, and walked through the chaos of life by my side; thank you. Thank you for the inside jokes, the long conversations, and the moments that made even the worst days bearable. Some of you have been constants, some of you have drifted in and out, but all of you have been a part of my story.

Friendships, like everything else in life, change. But if there's one thing I've learned, it's that the best ones aren't just about time, they're about the moments that felt like home. And to those who made me feel at home, even for a little while, I hope you know how much you meant to me.

To the people who became a part of my life and left their fingerprints behind, thank you for existing.

And to you, the one holding this book...
thank you for being here...

The Chronicles of Adi Murasaki

Aditya Udupa

BookLeaf Publishing

India | USA | UK

Presentation by *BookLeaf Publishing*

Web: www.bookleafpub.com

E-mail: info@bookleafpub.com

ISBN: 9789363312166

First edition 2024